This Is Poetry

Volume 2:
The Midwest Poets

Citizens for Decent Literature Press
a project of The Literary Underground

© Citizens for Decent Literature Press 2015

This Is Poetry
Volume II: The Midwest Poets

Editor:
Michele McDannold

Associate Editor:
James Griffin

Cover Art:
Michele McDannold

Cover Concept and Pictured on Front Cover:
Kat Spencer, Nostalgia Print

Photographer's Assistant:
Jason "Handyman" Watkins

ISBN-10: 0692495886
ISBN-13: 978-0692495889

All Rights Reserved. Printed in the United States of America.

also available from Citizens for Decent Literature Press:
This Is Poetry Volume I: Women of the Small Press

a project of The Literary Underground
theliteraryunderground.org

Many of the poems included in *This Is Poetry Volume II* are re-prints from the following publications and presses. The editors of this anthology wish to recognize and thank them for their contribution to the small press.

3:AM Magazine; Artists We Love; Atticus Review; BlazeVOX Books; Blotterature; Blue Root; Brickplight; The Camel Saloon; Chantarelle's Notebook; Cherry Bleeds; Chiron Review; Citizens for Decent Literature; Civil Coping Mechanisms; Connotation Press; ELJ Publications; every reason zine; Fox Chase Review; Grey Book Press; Gutter Eloquence Magazine; Horror, Sleaze, Trash; Huron River Review; Hyacinth Girl Press; Interior Noise Press; jenny; Laura Hird's Showcase; the lost beat; Lummox; The Momo Reader; My Favorite Bullet; NightBallet Press; Opium Poetry; OW III; Poetry Breakfast; ppigpenn; Punk Hostage Press; Red Fez Publications; Rural Messengers Press; Rusty Truck; Short, Fast, and Deadly; Side of Grits; Spirit Caller Magazine; Squares and Rebels Press; Steam Ticket Review; Terre Haute Poetry Asylum; Toledo Free Press Star; Underground Voices; Vintage Poetry; The Waterhouse Review; Wayne State Literary Journal; Wilderness House Review; Word Riot; and, Zygote in my Coffee.

CONTENTS

Catfish McDaris
   Lemons & Prairie Dogs ... pg 13
   We All Go Away Like An Echo Of Sad Laughter ... pg 14
   Van Gogh's Ear & The Low Riders Of El Paso Del Norte ... pg 15

April Michelle Bratten
   Lemon-Lime Refrigerator Cake ... pg 17

James Babbs
   Girl at the Gas Station ... pg 19
   Into the Wine ... pg 24
   The Smell of Burning Leaves ... pg 25

Michael D. Grover
   Gary Banfield ... pg 28
   Poetry Doesn't Suck People Do ... pg 29

Ryder Collins
   only you know i could never be a deerheart slayer ... pg 31

J.J. Campbell
   a long road to redemption ... pg 33
   this mystic ride ... pg 36
   the bitch with the black eye ... pg 38

CONTENTS

Susan Yount
Outages -- Cats -- Jobs -- Fiancés ... pg 40

Sirenna Blas
The Road is Real and You Are ... pg 43

Juliet Cook
Red Lunatic ... pg 45

Matthew Sradeja
The Eloquence ... pg 46
Dispersed ... pg 47
Little pink angels melt on my tongue ... pg 49

Judy L. Brekke
Dirt Road - 1960 ... pg 52

Wanda Morrow Clevenger
Summer Brimstone ... pg 54

Jake Russell
A Boy Meets His Muse ... pg 56
Teeth ... pg 57
The Shape of Dreams ... pg 58

David Blaine
Guns 'n Butter ... pg 59
That Human Disease ... pg 61

CONTENTS

David Blaine con't
 The Endless Pursuit ... pg 62
 The Usual Suspects ... pg 64

Michele McDannold
 Dear Baby Jesus ... pg 65
 Monkey Bars ... pg 69
 The Big Gulp ... pg 72

Craig Cady
 On Queer ... pg 74

Robert Vaughan
 Leaving ... pg 75
 Hummingbirds ... pg 76

Mark James Andrews
 Condoms on the Handlebars of a Rusted Bicycle ... pg 77
 As Midnight Fades into Dawn ... pg 78
 Revolution was about Pussy ... pg 79
 To Abstain ... pg 81

Josh Olsen
 Goldfish ... pg 82
 I Wish I Had a Camera ... pg 84
 A Sense of Humor ... pg 86
 You Burn Me ... pg 87

CONTENTS

Steven Gulvezan
　A Tooth for Shane MacGowan ... pg 88
　Walt Whitman at the Beach with a Martini ... pg 90

Trina Stolec
　One Closet ... pg 93

Cathleen Allyn Conway
　Motel Interlude ... pg 94

Joe Gianotti
　Washerwoman ... pg 95
　Late Night Burritos ... pg 97
　Grocery Girl ... pg 99

Bree
　when lost in innocence ... pg 100
　We Are All Orange ... pg 101

Ross Vassilev
　we'll be on our way home when the smoke whispers in the sky ... pg 104
　say what? ... pg 105
　semper fi ... pg 106
　trinity ... pg 108

CONTENTS

Scot Young
   Sunday Morning ... pg 110
   mother's bucket ... pg 112
   Poetry 101 ... pg 113

Walter Beck
   Generation Zero ... pg 115
   I Can Still See You (A Life of Dreams) ... pg 117
   The Wind Forgets My Name ... pg 118
   Death of a Generation ... pg 120

Justin Hyde
   3:38am at the truck stop ... pg 121
   the man in the back who ran the label machine ... pg 124
   grocery shopping for the schizophrenics ... pg 126

Brian Fugett
   Sheltering Sheila ... pg 127
   This is the Damn Poem ... pg 129
   Peristalsis in the Bowels of Downtown ... pg 130

Bill Yarrow
   The Deterioration of My Handwriting ... pg 132
   I Am Not a Corpse ... pg 134
   Before the Door ... pg 135

CONTENTS

Julie Demoff-Larson
You Should've Listened When I Told You Not to Play with Them Guns in the First Place ... pg 136
when you are a thousand miles from home ... pg 140

Tom Janikowski
crank ... pg 142
there have been better days ... pg 145

Kayla Greenwell
Practice ... pg 147

Tim Murray
Certified Outlaw ... pg 149
God Lost His Pet Gopher in a Patch of Roiling Gray Clouds Hovering Over Miller Beach Indiana ... pg 154
Part I ... pg 155

The Midwest Poets
Bios ... pg 158

"We die. That may be the meaning of life. But we do language. That may be the measure of our lives."

–Toni Morrison

Lemons & Prairie Dogs
Catfish McDaris

Most poetry sticks its
fingers down my throat
with nauseating boredom
& makes my teeth ache

I would rather
lick sunlight from a lemon
eat fragrance from a rose
drink blood from a pomegranate
hear crickets fiddle
watch stars vanish in mist

But a good poem is
lightning splitting an oak
a mountain of ebony basalt
butter melting on jalapeno cornbread
petrified wood
the Mona Lisa's smile
a prairie dog town

A tiger devouring
my mother.

We All Go Away Like An Echo Of Sad Laughter
Catfish McDaris

As I age I no longer wipe
away the tears, neither does
God, we watch the hungry on
the church steps searching
in the dirty melting snow.

Van Gogh's Ear & The Low Riders Of El Paso Del Norte
Catfish McDaris

Looking around at all the famous
Beatniks, I wondered why I'd been
invited to read & the flyer had my name

On the main night of three, a big
shot asked me out of the blue to
start the gig, I realized an ulterior
motive to my invitation

I'd been watching this young drummer
in the back of a pickup entertaining two
young Cherry Valley ladies, I asked him
to beat the conga while I did my thing

We found a bigger louder drum & he
started jackhammering a rhythm, I started
with a coyote whoophowl from the back
of the room making the audience turn if
they wanted to see me dance Apache

I woke up everyone screaming "This is for
the ear of Van Gogh & the lowriders in El Paso
del Norte, now let's limbo & get down"

Jumping on stage for the second poem, the
drum was beating that crowd into a frenzied
dervish, we had them in our palms & left
them all jonesing & wanting more

Sitting in the back, I wrote a poem about
when the Monkees asked Jimi Hendrix to
open for them & he started playing with
his teeth & set his guitar on fire.

Lemon-Lime Refrigerator Cake
April Michelle Bratten

She parted her mouth
into a disturbed flower,

red, white, wet,

and as cold as the refrigerator
she bent her hefty ass in front of.

She eyed my sad round face,
said I was only allowed to eat
one small piece

because girls aged 9
must watch their figures.

Her pregnant belly loomed before the pan
like a tarred-out sun,
a big black disaster,

as she scooped out
my tiny jiggling serving.

It moved like jelly, like
her thighs, underarms, and neck.

It moved like the ocean I knew so well.

The soft cake
was cold in my mouth.

It was the snow-covered prairie I had yet to see.
It was the owl hooting above my quiet tent many years after that.
It was the wedding dress that I never wanted to wear.
It was a small apartment, an Irish man, and the New York City skyline.

With my fork, I quickly swiped
another sliver from the pan
and popped it into my mouth
while her flabby back was turned.

It was the cold rain pouring from a roof to calm my bare feet.
It was the green sky before the big tornado of 2001.
It was the white window dressing of the Hotel Buckminster.
It was a highway, paper, wine, and Lake Pontchartrain Bridge.

My young mouth sucked at the future.

Hey! she suddenly screamed,
slamming her fist on the old wooden table.

I said just one.

Girl at the Gas Station
James Babbs

    i.
the girl at
the gas station
emerges from
the storeroom
fighting hiccups
and
she laughs
says
excuse me
and
I do
because she's
beautiful

    ii.
when the girl at
the gas station
laughs
it reminds me
of the chimes
hanging in
the tree
outside
my bedroom
window
I think
the people

next door
put them there

    iii.
the girl at
the gas station
has several
piercings in
her ears
wears earrings
matching
the stud in
her nose and
when she
opens her mouth
I see
the metal in
her tongue
wondering
what else
she has pierced
but I'm
too afraid
to ask

    iv.
the girl at
the gas station
says
good afternoon
at the same time

I say
how are you
so that
our voices
cancel
each other
out

    v.
the girl at
the gas station
stocks cigarettes
from behind
the counter
her back to me
when I
come in

    vi.
the girl at
the gas station
knows my name
because
I always
use my
credit card
and sign
the receipt but
don't know hers
because
she never

wears her
name tag and
everyone
even
the old women
just call her
beautiful

    vii.
the girl at
the gas station
argues with
somebody on
the phone as
I stand there
waiting and
she says
asshole
before slamming
down the phone
turning to me
all smiles

    viii.
the girl at
the gas station
has never
been married
but
somebody told me
she has

a child
and if
that's true
so what

    ix.
the girl at
the gas station
isn't
the same girl
from yesterday
but
she smiles
doesn't seem to
mind being
someone else

Into the Wine
James Babbs

and it already feels like
it's too late
not even dark yet and
I've started on the second bottle
because the first one
didn't make my feel any better
I keep trying to call her
but she doesn't answer me
almost the new year and
I hope to get drunk
more than I do now
when I stand in the living room
and look down the hallway
I can see the picture of Jesus
leaning against the wall
his hands in the air
and he's out on the water
before it was mine
the picture belonged to my mother
I remember it
hanging out on the porch
right above the freezer
it's cold in here and
I can't write anymore
I'm not as young as I used to be

The Smell of Burning Leaves
James Babbs

I recognized her
when I saw her coming toward me
walking slowly across the yard
I hadn't seen her for a long time
but she looked about the same to me
just a little older around the eyes
with a sprinkle of gray in her hair
I'd read about her son's death
a couple of days ago in the paper
he was serving in the military and
wouldn't be coming back home
what are you up to
she said
I saw the trace of a smile on her face
I said
just trying to get the yard cleaned up
you know
burning some leaves
I saw her glance at the fire
I said
I'm sorry about your son
because I didn't know what else to say
she looked at the ground
Keith loved the smell of burning leaves
she said
she looked at the fire again
she said
he always did

even when he was little
I looked at the pile of leaves near my feet
at the trash can I was using to
carry the leaves over to the fire
I said
yeah me too
but it sounded really dumb
she touched my arm
but only for a second
I said
so how are you doing
she closed her eyes before answering
as good as I can be
she said
I said
that's all we can do
isn't it
the wind suddenly shifted and
the smoke from the burning leaves
drifted toward us
we wallowed in the silence for several moments
she said
well
I'll let you get back to work
I just saw you out here
and thought I'd come say hello
I said
I'm glad you did
she stepped toward me and
gave me a hug
I said

take care of yourself
when she pulled herself away from me
she said
I have to
and I watched her walk away
but then she stopped and
turned back toward me and
gave me a wave
I waved back at her
before I picked up the trash can and
started dumping more leaves on the fire

Gary Banfield
Michael D. Grover

Used to be a punk rocker
He joined the marines
Fought in desert storm
One night not long after he got back
I saw him at Respectables Street Cafe
He was sitting at the bar with his head down
So I asked him what was troubling him
I have nothing here Mike, I can't find a job or anything
Plus they did something to us in that war
My nerves are shot
I have dreams of killing people
I have dreams of killing myself
I want to kill everybody
It's not right Mike
They will not even acknowledge there is something wrong with me
Everyone knows they used nerve gas on us
Not everyone knew, but I knew
I didn't really know what to say
I just looked at him, *You really don't want to kill anyone*
He said he wanted to kill everyone
That every day he stuck his gun in his own mouth
All I could say was *That really sucks man*
He nodded & agreed

Poetry Doesn't Suck People Do
Michael D. Grover

All of the time I hear how Poetry sucks
In grandiose all knowing articles,
Fahey shouts it from the big stage
Poetry sucks
Like a whore out in the neighborhood,
Like a vacuum,
Like depression on the state of the human race
Poetry sucks
Now they bury her again, and again
Poetry dead with a single ice pick hole
Naked her porcelain, translucent skin
Glowing in the moonlight
Her beautiful naked body covered in blood
A nook crammed up her ass
Poetry sucks
In a World of image without substance
Poetry sucks
In a World of snake oil businessmen
Poetry sucks
I go to coffee shops
And crazy empty bars to hear her
I so rarely find her anymore
Poetry sucks
I still host readings in her name
Poetry sucks
I read tens of thousands of
Submissions for free
Just so that I can find her

And create something beautiful
Poetry sucks
I have traveled from city to city
To see her
& I know where her heart is
I know who my kin are
Poetry sucks
Under a generic blanket of PC niceness
With no soul
Poetry sucks
As I read & create it
Poetry doesn't suck
People do
I saw her get up and walk away
From the whole scene
She wakes me up at four thirty in the morning
& fucks the shit out of me
Poetry doesn't suck
People do

only you know i could never be a deerheart slayer
Ryder Collins

the old mens follow me down grocery aisles. they say, northern girl, how about some canned beets? they say, northern girl, look at this cucumber, they say, northern girl, northern girl, they say, share some Black Jack gum & your hoochie with us. then they unzip their trousers and these guys are so old nothing keeps them up and they're wearing sock garters and spats. that's when i runs from them & they say, that old skidoo... that old skidoo.

you know i'm good at giving the old skidoo.

you taught me all the moves.

& maybe later i'll go tease those old guys at the vfw. it's just up the road. maybe i'll run into the woodsman first & he'll hand me a locked box with bambi's heart in it. then i can play. then i can take bambi's heart & hand it to the next mans and say, look, i give you this. and the mans won't know any better, & then i'll laugh a wicked queen laugh.

it will reverberate through deerheart chambers

it will reverberate through woodsmanheart chambers & valves even

it will reverberate through

it will reverb

1-2-3-4

still

once i counted your chambers; once i counted your heartbeats every night. felt your heart slowing, palm outstretched on your chest, my fingers longgrasping over sinews and skin for something you said or something you hid or something you never had but wanted all along yet

a long road to redemption
J.J. Campbell

i'm slowly drowning here in my
inability to chase away my past

my cousin's teenage nipples
in my mouth at age four

my father's hands wrapped
around my neck as i prayed
to pass out and die

the first time i got a rope, a
ladder and thought about
climbing a tree

the night i drank a bottle of
nyquil and decided to light
a bonfire

the smell of burning flesh
is still fresh in my mind

the joy of being the white kid
in my part black part nigger
part white childhood in a
forgotten suburb

to finding the right one only to
find out that she likes girls

to finding the other right one
only to realize that you work
better together as friends

that is until the fiancé is
uncomfortable with the
knowledge that the best
friend once had his dick
in the soon to be wife's ass

drinking and driving

searching for a cheap thrill

an easy whore that can cough

a gun that won't get jammed

but this solitary road is filled
with forks and you can rest
assured i've taken nothing but
wrong paths

the therapy never worked

the alcohol turned into torture
for pleasure

and i'm too poor to afford the drugs

closing in on thirty

my hope is fading like paint on
a car deserted in the sun

it's a long road to redemption when
you have no fucking desire to walk
the path at all

let alone trying to do it with only
the help of past demons, yes people
and fellow tortured souls that
wouldn't mind a death sealed with
hollywood approval

thank god i was blessed with good
looks, an athletic body and a silver
spoon in my mouth

fuck

that's my imaginary friend of my
youth i'm thinking of

i bet that fucker still gets more
pussy than me

the bastard

didn't even have the courtesy to take
me along when he made his escape

this mystic ride
J.J. Campbell

come find me
resting peacefully
in a crease of
time

come find me
placing my lips
gently on yours

take me with
a teenager's
desire

the urgency to
believe nothing
matters after
this night

this moment

this final act
of desperation
thought to be
reserved for
someone
better

may we find

serenity holy
and true while
dancing upon
this mystic ride

into a future
that includes
neither of us

the bitch with the black eye
J.J. Campbell

watching the local
evening news when
a woman with a
black eye comes
on and talks about
a hit and run accident
on her street

i said that must be on
the east side of town

and my sister looks
up and says hold up,
ain't no one gonna
say shit about the
bitch with the black
eye

and i laughed, said
it's pretty obvious
she only had to be
told once

and my mother
laughed

it's good to know
where i get my

sick sense of
humor from

and it's always
good when a
domestic violence
joke brings the
family closer
together

Outages – Cats – Jobs – Fiancés
Susan Yount

As a child I thought my parents
wore human masks.

Once, during a storm, a white ball of lightning
entered our house. We're not sure from where;
we were watching TV. It was the size of a fist
and seemed to last for 20 seconds. No matter
where it went, the cat was in front. She pissed
a trail and led the ball onto the sofa where it
disappeared, leaving a foul, rotten egg smell.

The cat's name was Samantha. She was
my first cat. I cut off her whiskers.
She still slept with me afterwards.

My second cat's name was Bandit; she kept a black eye.

When I was in grade school, I was afraid
to tell the truth so lied about everything.
Everyone told me I'd be a great actress.
I had lead rolls in several school plays.

I was a latch key kid and once after the bus
dropped me off, I watched a tornado rip the roof
from our barn throwing hay miles.

I was with my neighbor and best friend when
her mother kidnapped her. She was so excited

she didn't even say goodbye.

In Junior High I told everyone my real name was Samantha.

At 16, a tarot card reader, whom I paid with cartons
of Camels, three rolled joints and once a bottle of Cisco
told me I'd get everything I worked for. Each time
he read cards for me he would sigh and say, *see there*.
After the third reading he handed me the Tarot
of the Cat People and quit reading cards completely.

I knew I wouldn't marry my first fiancé but said yes anyway.

On our first date it was raining and I pulled
a kitten from his storm drain. I named it Mouse.

My senior year in high school, I told my flag choir
director a rumor that his wife, my drama teacher,
was having an affair with a friend of mine.
It turned out true. I haven't acted since.

My first fiancé took me to see a local prophet.
Upon entering her house she yelled *FIRE*.
My first fiancé and I asked if she was OK.
She acted like she hadn't said anything.
Later that night she grabbed my arm,
*It is you, you're a fireball yet I see you
leading people away from a fire*. I never
went back to her house nor saw her again.

I knew I wouldn't marry my second fiancé but said yes anyway.

He was a loser drug dealer convicted felon on parole. I knew
he would save me or kill me. The cards, the tattoos said so.
He threatened both. I wanted to be a photographer or a poet.

When I was 20 I lost my mind. I was still living
with my parents working full-time nights in a factory,
part-time afternoons waitressing and part-time college.
I did that for four months and then I was pulled over
on a back road state road doing 90 between jobs.
I quit everything to color coloring books. I wouldn't
speak. I was a ghost for weeks. My mother sobbed
and threatened to take me to Life Springs.

Though I didn't call in sick to either job, both called
wanting me back. I returned only to the factory.
The next day I wanted to leave my second fiancé;
I was standing next to him when his best friend shot him.
That night, police took him away. In prison, he got gangrene.

I knew I would marry my third fiancé so said no
to the third man who asked me to marry him.

I taught him everything about violence and living
and death and he waited 6 years to offer anything.
When he did, it wasn't real. My next cat's

name was Mimi. She hated me at first but loved
me later. She belonged to my third fiancé. We quit
smoking together. He likes opera and we travel well.

The Road is Real and You Are
Sirenna Blas

They are hyacinth girls in springtime—the usual dancing
in rain that young girls are fond of, shaking water off their
ballet flats in front of the boys, wringing the water
from each other's hair. Girls who
create secrets just to burn them beneath trapdoors,
who write poetry across their breasts for art, who take people in
but don't realize how they burn them.
And they'll say they're raw,
but they're only sleepy flowers, the kind that if
you scratch your nail down the petal, you leave
a watery mark behind. But,

in the winter,
they learn to drive the roads like madmen.
It's all eyes, ass, feet, mind, how hands become a compass
and tongues, the map back home. It is
a love affair between Girl
and machine, Girl
and the ladies in the backseat, Girl
and the way things blur past at her own command.

The street unfurls from your palm like soaked, black ribbon,
feel it,
and there is nothing but to tug harder
until it coils back inside of you,
rebirth it.
Denounce the decorum, sweethearts—

the road is real and you are

forever in its debt, not
the boys', nor the images', and never the flowers'
which you have painted onto yourselves that try to root
into concrete porches. Your skin might become the concrete
one day,
your feet the pressure that compels you to move,
but not the porch, nor burnt paper, and never
the rooms beneath trapdoors.

Red Lunatic
Juliet Cook

Loony bin pyrotechnics glimmer
inside my disaster zone, call me
a new sort of sizzling underwater forensic science;
what will you find deep down here?
Will red fins bramble or writhe open

a snake hissing into Bloodybelly Comb Jelly.

I tried to turn burn marks into sticky drizzles
but my whip-poor-will songs oozed out red pussy
willow nightmares. I did not wish for red devil centers
with the last of the turquoise eggs falling out; cracking.
My wisdom teeth never grew to replace those holes.

The Eloquence
Matthew Sradeja

It seems so simple
The idea illuminated
In the mind
Like dust fluttering
In the waning sunbeams
Stretched across the dining room
At the end of the day

Real long thoughts
But, I have to pause

The smell of banana bread
Baking makes the cut up
Watermelon
Blush

I begin to wonder
Do I have the
Eloquence?
To put the thought out there?
In the mosaic air
Where

Some will see sky colored mortar and
Cloud colored stones

While others will see cloud colored
Mortar and sky colored stones

And I might never know

Dispersed
Matthew Sradeja

Ain't that the truth
I would say that
Damn near everything
That can be dispersed
Has been spread thin
As thin as the single ply toilet paper
At just about every rest stop
Between here and east Jesus
For Christ sake
And paper
Ain't the half of it
Shit, shit is what we pass
Through the system
And call it money
We bleed money
We do
You can call it
Commerce or capitalism
Call it rainbow bright
If that is what gets you through the night
Dispersed is what you get
When the union and the company
Can't get a decent contract together
And the pain is felt on the factory floor
I'd say the shit has been dispersed
Pretty damned well enough
When the chairman of the union committee
Packs up his tools in the night and walks away

There must be something dragging him away
From his union brothers
Lord knows what it could be

Little pink angels melt on my tongue
Matthew Sradeja

I have trouble sleeping
so I take melatonin,
it doesn't work very well,
so I take Ambien too.
Winding down and passing out
in the middle of a famous poem
only does the job if I have a fan on
for the sound and the breeze

All the fans are too loud
so I wear ear plugs.
I have high triglycerides
I get that from my mother's side
of the family
I take Antara for that
and fish oil too.

My sugar is elevated
I am borderline diabetic
I am supposed to stay away
from eating carbohydrates
but, I love pancakes
and every other kind of cake.
I take fiber to stay regular
and driving, working, waiting in line,
Eating out, and being around people
in general
practically everything gives me

high anxiety.
I take Xanax for that,
I love Xanax,
those little pink angels melt on my tongue..

Nothing
brightens my dreamscapes
like Xanax.

I see crowds of people
burning like wild fire,
tornadoes of wrath,
blurring the lines
and blocking out
my sense of self.

Thanks to Xanax
I don't ever mind it
not even a fly wing width.

Every night I dance in a concrete jungle
hungry for steel to slam
into steel.
Listening to the
industrial pneumatics breathing
life into the mechanical genius
of a twenty five thousand ton press
roaring into the future.
Always the future with xanax,
never the past, the bloated dead
corpse, the past.

The eagle bone and chicken feather
dance in the past.

I barely ever notice it.
Dogs howl and trains
moan into the night
and I pretend it is all
alright.

Little pink angels melt on my tongue
and night shaded devils
nod approval to my every action
so long as I don't look back.

Dirt road - 1960
Judy L. Brekke

walking down dirt road
bordered by cattails
rattling in wind
gravel poking bottom
of flip flops

chew fingernails
on stubby fingers
ignore parents bribe
of $1.00 for each
nail that grows

rusted red pick-up
drives erratically
dirt, dust, and gravel
spit from beneath
tread-worn tires

shotgun on back window
straw hat angled on driver's head
he looks in side mirror
slows, stops truck
flicks half smoked cigarette out window

into moist swamp
hide amongst crackling cattails
black muck and lime green algae
squeeze between toes

hungry gnats buzz head

driver turns his head
of shaggy blond hair
checks dust covered
rear view mirror
truck starts

rusted red truck
spins wheels
spats gravel
cigarette smoke billows
out window

back on dirt road
mud covered feet
speckled with green
neck full of gnat bites
no fingernails to chew

mom and dad will understand

Summer Brimstone
Wanda Morrow Clevenger

Revivals were held
at the fairgrounds in the '60s;
7 nights in 80 degree summer
fired up long before sunset

officiated by some hotshot
from somewhere else brought in
to shake the roof because bland
falls short; is spit out
quicker than stale saltines

the hotshots came
to save us from ourselves
mostly filling hardwood
bleachers reserved
for horse race, demo derby
and kiddie pageant; we faithful
fanning Sunday Best dry

behind the stage salvation
a freight train jiggled the horizon;
I counted the mismatched boxcars
before a bored boy began scooting nearer

and caught at this kind of thing
at revival
calls down worse brimstone
than any preacher guesses;

I looked away and wished for
another train to roll by.

A Boy Meets His Muse
Jake Russell

A fire-pit does celebrate
the end of summer. We're convinced
that August doesn't finish.
The smoke does not dissuade
mosquitoes sucking

a boy toward a toilet,
who's buried
under the influence of
Kinnell and Young.
The boy opens the door to

a "Just a moment" shame;
a girl is perched
on spotless porcelain.
She smiles forgiveness
and afterward she strolls from

his life forever.

Teeth
Jake Russell

I've heard the rumor:
you like to eat hearts for natural protein:
mix 'em with au gratin broccoli
and chew methodically,

but your teeth are a reminder
as to how I failed Margaret,
and how Margaret was mistreated
by so many guys,

and I was one of them
because I led her on.
I was young, but innocence
never acquits my regret, so

I will let your teeth paralyze
as they bite my leg.
If your tongue moves to my chest —
well, I shouldn't be surprised.

The Shape of Dreams
Jake Russell

The first pig to fly is wiped
out by an airplane.
Bacon rains the neighborhood.

A second pig cloud devours its airplane.
By the third pig, the dream is achieved,
the tinkering pays off — wah lah! — to functioning

machines. If these shapes in the clouds actually
meant anything, I'd have it fucking made.

Guns 'n Butter
David Blaine

I'd been having an affair
with a hydrocarbon medusa.

A crude relationship
based on heavy metal
M.R.E.'s and gunshot residue.

I wanted her to meet the folks
but she couldn't come inside,

said their roof blocked out the sky,
said she could only climax
on her back
with starlight glancing
off the soles of her feet.

At water's edge
Medusa pulled me atop of her.
But as I plunged in she was cut
on a scrap of beach glass.

She bled out on the sand
and left me lying in a pool
of thirty weight.

A classic conundrum.

It was infatuation;

I couldn't get enough of her.
But my mother is happier now.
She says a hydrocarbon medusa
was too old for me anyway.

That Human Disease
David Blaine

I remember

the old man's lap
a comfortable perch
for a toddler.

We watched the game
in black and white
on a blond Emerson.

He drank Ballantine Ale
from a glass
and I got to take
a foamy sip once
in a while.

He smoked a cigar
or puffed Cherry Blend
in his pipe and I shared
both with him,
through osmosis.

That was fifty years ago—
He's been gone a good twenty.

Now I smoke and drink
too much
and I should probably quit, but
I just can't seem to let go of him yet.

The Endless Pursuit
David Blaine

With the last of the purple skylight
come certain private conversations

birds fall silent in the gloaming
like a flute fading away
at a life-or-death moment.

This is no whispered romance
but excess baggage:

the promise of a card from Budapest
left over from his panicked days

a fifty franc note
the only residual good will.

You'd offered yourself—
the first buckling bloom in spring snow

only to be blown across the yard
like last year's leaves
bagged and dragged to the curb.

But just as ice eventually recedes
your blossom continues to unfold.

The man with the jumping frogs
will tell you

any standing water
eventually bubbles with tadpoles

and a wise Spanish seductress
should continue to do her own thing.

The Usual Suspects
David Blaine

Because they are the hands that sign the orders
Because they are the hands that pull the trigger
Because they are the hands that wipe our shitty asses
Because they are the hands that groped your sister's tits

Because they are the hands that strike our children
Because they, too, are the hands of Brutus
Because they are the hands that deal in currency
Because they are the dealer's hands

Because they are the hands that fill the needle
Because they are the hands that heat the spoon
Because they are the hands that push the big red button
Because they are the hands that pull the final switch

Because they are the hands that swing the hammer
Because they are the hands that place the nails

Because they are the hands of Judas, pointing
Because they are our thumbs upon the scale

Because they are the hands that take and
the hands that refuse to give

Because they are all our hands
Because they are the hands of all
Because we   are the usual suspects.

Dear Baby Jesus
Michele McDannold

Thank you for the best childhood ever
for the nicely manicured lawns
dutifully tended to every Sunday
after church
for the sun tea baking on the porch
and the strawberries in the patch
Thank you, baby jesus
for the community free of minorities
and forward thinking
for the streets free of gang violence
for the jehovah's witness even
and the evangelists
thank you for putting the shame on
all those unwed and/or single mothers
those people with the weak-minded mental illnesses
and the ghastly homosexuals
in general, just thank you so much
for putting a clamp down
on all the SEX stuff
I didn't know what my period was
until I got it one day in gym
that kinda sucked
but thank you
and maybe while you were hiding
all the dildos and other adult fun
you could have taught the old people
not to stick their fingers and whatnot
in the young people

that would have been nice
but oh well
maybe that's why Billy Bob's uncle
is also his dad
I never met anyone conceived from incest before
COOL
thank you, baby jesus

I know. I know
some people want to give all the credit to Satan
Lucifer
the Devil
whatever
he's busy with wars
tsunamis
and shit
he wants the glory of all those big fatality numbers
you... you are oh so patient
killing them softly and gently
with shitty lives
contrived of stifling rules...
call it morality!
Shame, shame
the bent and twisted
call it love
BABY JESUS
I want you to have all the credit
saving us all from the fires of Hell

I can pray to you for forgiveness
I can pray to you for the Friday night football game

we can all join hands and pray pray pray
then sing the star spangled banner
oh, thank you, baby jesus
for making me an American
thank you for making us better
than every other nation in the world
so what if we drop the ball
in our schools
turn our backs
on mother nature
and would turn out
anyone or anything
in the best interest
of the almighty dollar

we are responsible for FACEBOOK
Honey Boo Boo
and taco shells made out of Doritos!
this is all thanks to you, baby jesus

but, wait...
I have more rights to my guns
than my own body!!
sweet baby jesus
thank you
oh, thank you
for Women that know their place
in dresses
in kitchens
in the delivery room
children, children, children

let's have more babies, baby jesus!
Every last one of them, precious
until they learn to breathe
in the polluted
but free as all fuck
liberty-laced air

Monkey Bars
Michele McDannold

Isn't it
just a bit
usual these days
to be talking
shit, fuck?
I was reading this novel
by this great guy
'so and so',
it was only
a few years back,
and it actually said
shit fuck,
shit fuck.
Then later on
when I was reading
some other stuff–
poetry and the like,
well,
I had really
noticed
lots of cunts
for some reason
I've never really
cared for that word,
and don't use it myself,
but back to shit fuck
it's losing power these days
it used to turn heads

even my mother
doesn't flinch anymore
when I let it slip
...fucking shit.

It started for me
on the playground,
a game with Tracey,
the toughest girl in town
who I wanted to be
and Jeff,
the dirtiest boy
in town
who I wanted,
even in Grade 3.
man, don't tell me
we're not born with it.
so I learned all my
shit fuck
bastard, piss
on the monkey bars
but I never really
perfected it
until the year I worked
in that slaughterhouse.
I was nineteen and desperate.
everyone there was desperate,
shit fuck, became—
"I ain't takin'
no fuckin' shit
piss off, bitch

suck my dick."
It became
an art form
and second nature.
I know at times
you gotta keep it in check
and I do try
to tone it down
but damnit,
it's sewn deep
and when people keep talking
shit fuck, shit fuck,
sometimes,
I hate to hear others say it
sounds cheap,
`cause baby,
it comes at a price.

The Big Gulp
Michele McDannold

About living in vegas...
for the first three weeks,
we lived in a week to week
rental
it was—how shall I say,
questionable.

if you hear screaming,
do not come running.
happen to have a phone
call 911.
'course,
rooms don't come equipped
good luck finding a pay phone
with receiver still attached.

there was a pool though
there is not a hotel/motel/condo/shack
rental of any kind
in vegas that does not have a pool.
I think it's the law.
and, yes.
it had water.
and it was clean.
during the morning hours
when the bulk of the undesirables
were sleeping it off
or still kickin' it, but so fucked

they couldn't be of any real harm
I went swimming
it was bliss.

I don't care what anyone says
about dry heat
115 degrees
is 115 degrees
you sweat your ass off
it just evaporates so fast
it doesn't have time to collect
thank god for 7-11 and the big gulp
if it wasn't for the pool
7-11 and their big gulp,
99 cent shrimp cocktails
down on Freemont street...
free spaghetti dinners
from that trashy casino
with the penny slots,
I never would have made it
those first three weeks.
I never would have hocked
everything I owned to stay on.

On Queer
Craig Cady

the Radical Anything//gay as fuck swishing
down midwest streets kissing yr friends &
Acceptance-inclusion even
the str8s who look on
w/that weird longing at times
& they're us too(, I guess & not)--
a.) Queer:::a.) Minority of
LOVE damaged tragically sometimes always conceptual
from lqqks to showshowshows way more apt to fuck
in groups//all our naked friends
a knowing an awareness an understood glance on the bus

on the bus we take the bus

Shane Shane's asshole//Dusty's beard a cunt beat exploration
that discordant
composition Lucas Carey made about Kafka the intimacy we
share
you don't have to have sex & if you're compulsive
about it we get it & if you want to wear
that thing in public we definitely get it
& we'll help you make it & build a stage

Leaving
Robert Vaughan

Leaving: a cadence, a beat.
Repetition in our minds, lost and forgotten.
A shoe box empty and discarded. Painful, stumbling through, not around, this hurdle.
And still, caresses linger at the bottom of this bag of memories like a boulder.
Leaving: a door closes on feelings, darker out there. Blackness, but somehow enables me to shine.
From this dark hallway I see roses in the moonlight.
The soft streetlight against the stars.
They have not forgotten me.
Upon leaving, a self-conscious, thwarted, last attempt to grasp a passing wave. Ride it to the shore:
A failed attempt.
A deep sense of false pride. An aching troubled fit creeps along the path to the street.
The front yard screams at you.
And the car.
And the buttons on your shirt.
Leaving: Yes, I am leaving.
Still, you might have the chance to get there before me.

Hummingbirds
Robert Vaughan

The day is carved out like a pumpkin, slit open for visitors. My question is when am I perfect, and will you be looking the other way? Here is a sparrow bone to stand in for me. Carry it like the look you gave me when you wanted me naked in meadows under the meteorites.

Tonight we miss the moment to marry, the ring slipping into an imperceptible freedom as we spiral into our own potential. Why do you say it's too dangerous? It's like any slide, like any roller-coaster, you're strapped in, here we are hands- free, watch me! What is danger anyhow?

Over breakfast this morning, Dana told me hummingbirds represent the number eight, infinity. Their wings flapping so quickly they create this symbol. They dart, and dance and one even perched on an inert limb. I told her I'd heard a story once in which a hummingbird went crazy on an intruder. Within a second, poked both his eyes out.

We've been here before, you and me, haven't we? The first time we danced in a fist of a writhing crowd. The first time we kissed in a bowl of neglect. If we could take into consideration how many lives our thoughts and actions impact? Now I know I see you everywhere as if you've flown away, and looped back a hundred times.

Condoms on the Handlebars of a Rusted Bicycle
Mark James Andrews

three sneakers are dangling
from the braided fiber optic line parabola
pole to pole in the sky
as we crash over pothole craters
in the pod of a restored rear-engine
Volkswagen Beetle on a back street
that looks like Dresden after World War 2
as we disembark into a forbidden quadrant
to poke gingerly with salvaged pool cues
from a fire bombed corner whiskey bar
at burial mounds in this artifact rich
free garage and yard sale
in abandoned homesteads
and hulks of chop shopped automobiles
as we recall biblical Noah
with his white dove and olive branch
but drunk and naked in a tent at the end
while we separate clothing
from data cable and cobbles from
condoms on the handlebars of a rusted bicycle
in glory where the grips should be.

As Midnight Fades into Dawn
Mark James Andrews

I am staying tuned
to the big rug top man
as he leads me
thru the moral distinctions
between killing and murder
and just when he is beating
the fine points to death ha ha
his timing kicks in
and he shifts into overdrive
into a concept he calls Chrislam
foreshadowing his grand wrap-up
end times end times glory glory
as the camera keeps cutting away
to quick shots of his adoring wife
waiting in the wings
to belt out a spiritual
her wig hat is a bit off kilter
but that lipstick mouth
really delivers the message.

Revolution was about Pussy
Mark James Andrews

Revolution was about pussy
more pussy
strange pussy
better drugs
more drugs
a free spot to crash

All night strategy sessions
Mao's red book
working Che into the conversation
nodding to the awful obvious music
these rituals were to be practiced
to be endured.

The worst were the mass movements
the tribal gatherings
sit-ins were preferable
to the awful marching
the signs and slogans
chanting in unison.

And now wandering this Occupation
Grand Circus Park in the 3-1-3
faces are again young & sensual
slumming & kinky in tent city
a new wisdom permeates
ignore organization
abandon philosophy.

A sleeping bag is hung in the wind
bodily fluids are drying
a young male in a Sherpa hat
sidles up to a young female
bowing to cell phone texting
silently weighing his chances.

To Abstain
Mark James Andrews

To abstain is less welcome than death
and so I lay in piss strong alleyways
while you try to tell me what is real

Goldfish
Josh Olsen

My son won a goldfish at the carnival.

Actually, I bought my son a goldfish at the carnival.

The game cost three dollars to play, but if you paid five you got a fish, win or lose, and so of course I paid five.

I paid another five dollars for an inflatable sword, seven dollars for a small stuffed puppy, and twenty for a plush Smurf, and then my son and I walked home in the dark, the chaos of the over-attended carnival fading into luscious silence.

I felt drunk with love for my child as he sang and skipped and danced down the sidewalk, and I wished that it would be moments like this that he remembered when he looked back on his childhood.

And then, less than three blocks from home, the glow of our porchlight visible in the near distance, he shit his pants.

He instantly began to cry as diarrhea ran down his legs, into his socks and brand new sneakers, and I realized then that, without a doubt, he would most certainly remember this night for a long, long time.

When we got home, his mother stripped him of his heavy, soiled clothes and lifted him into the shower while I delicately transferred the goldfish into a glass vase.

More than anything else, I feared that the goldfish would immediately die and punctuate the night with a perfect symphony of sorrow, but it did not.

It lived and thrived in that very vase that eventually was moved from my son's bedroom to my office desk, and it wasn't soon after that my son wanted a puppy, and KT and I decided to get him one from the pound, and once that was said and done I might as well have flushed the goldfish down the toilet.

But I didn't.

I Wish I Had a Camera
Josh Olsen

"I wish I had a camera," I said in reaction to the seemingly thousands of birds perched on the power-lines running parallel to the Detroit House of Corrections.

How could I write about them without coming off cliché, without sounding "cheesy" while writing about the juxtaposition of flight and imprisonment?

I knew a picture would be the only way to capture the moment.

I couldn't write about it, I'd only abstract it...by changing the time of day or season, by ignorantly using my limited knowledge of birds to name them incorrectly, by calling them cardinals or blackbirds.

Or by not making them birds, at all.

By changing them to pumpkins or tigers, or making the prison a carnival.

On Haggerty Rd was a dump that housed old concession trailers, large rusted boxes advertising corn dogs, funnel cakes, and elephant ears.

That'd make a great setting for a poem!

"I wish I had a camera," I said, and asked KT whose permission I'd need to be granted access into the decrepit, condemned prison.

KT assumed the institution was maximum security, "Because of all the concertina wire," she said, and I laughed at her choice of words – "Razor-wire, you mean?"

Concertina didn't sound like something created to tear human skin, it sounded too sweet, like Italian spun sugar.

I imagined the inmates licking their way to freedom – the fence melting on their tongues.

"I wish I had a camera," I said, curling my fingers into the fence, momentarily unclear on which side of it I stood.

A Sense of Humor
Josh Olsen

I bought two children's frozen dinners and a fifth of Smirnoff vodka, which was reasonably priced, but still more expensive than the two frozen dinners combined.

"Wife's bringing the kids over tonight," I joked with the cashier, but she didn't find it funny.

She peered down at my ring finger, conspicuously absent of a wedding band, and shot me a look of quiet consternation.

Some people were born without a sense of humor.

You Burn Me
Josh Olsen

In white spray paint, lengthwise upon the green overpass, were the words, *I apologize*, and over it, in dripping pink brush strokes, *YOU BURN ME*.

A man was dropping garbage onto traffic below.

An overripe pineapple exploded on the windshield of a Dodge Caravan, while a sticky nine of spades with a pink fingerprint in the center adhered to mine.

"Is this your card?" I imagined the man on the overpass asking, but before I could respond, he jumped.

A Tooth for Shane MacGowan
Steven Gulvezan

His gums bled sorrow that night
A bit unsteady
Sunglasses
Cigarette up and down
Big orange drink
Placed carefully on a stool
He confronted the microphone
"When I first came to London I was only sixteen…"

The boozy beery crowd of soul searchers
Hungry for something
A young woman opened on violin
Short skirt
Long legs
Supple
The way she became one
With her instrument

Black suit stained with unknown
Excrement he tightened erect
The pulse of the music and the
Push of so many bodies thrust
Him back to the city the streets
Grey smoke swirling street lights
Dirty yellow through the haze
"Kissed my girl by the factory wall…"

Some hero surrendered a tooth

To the lip of a bottle
Held it high
The crowd went wild
Some punk accosted a wily old sport
The old sport smiled
Clocked the punk cleanly
The crowd went wild

Tears in an old man's beer
He waxed sentimental
And looked upon this family of friends
Linked arms swaying
As they sang to his tune
And shared his sorrow
To survive one more night
"And a-rovin' a-rovin' a-rovin' I'll go…"

Walt Whitman at the Beach with a Martini
Steven Gulvezan

It took me three days
To get my biography
Exactly correct
I sifted through my memories
Selecting the quirky
And unusual jobs I held
Many years ago
When I was young
While conveniently forgetting
The mundane position
Which has put bread on my table
For thirty years

I revised amusing anecdotes
About my life
That reveal my rebellious self
In all my James Dean glory

I leafed through my collection
Of photographs of famous writers
So many looks to choose from
Edgar Allen Poe
Dylan Thomas
The young Ernest Hemingway
The middle-aged Ernest Hemingway
The old Ernest Hemingway
Allen Ginsberg
And Raymond Carver

Through a process of trial and error
I created a sort of mélange
Deciding that the hairstyle
Of Gertrude Stein in Paris
While she pondered
Exactly what a rose was
Above the spectacles
Of James Joyce in Switzerland
Just before he went almost completely blind
And the smile of Malcolm Lowry
Gin bottle in his hand
Posing outside his shack at Dollarton
Shortly before it burned down
Surrounded by the beard of Walt Whitman
Blowing in the wind
On some misty Manhattan street corner
Gave me the look of a man possessed
By genius

Next I bought my wife a camera
And posed for her all weekend
Sitting in an outdoor café
That could pass for the Riviera
Sipping a martini
A la F. Scott Fitzgerald
Waving goodbye
From a walkway
Similar to the Washington Avenue Bridge
That John Berryman jumped off of
And standing in the sand

Not unlike the Tangier
Beatnik beach
Of William S. Burroughs

Under my direction
My wife
Clicked the shutter
Perhaps a thousand times

I scrutinized the photos
Until I finally found one
That revealed
The true, absolute, inner me

All that's left for me to do
Is take an hour or two
To knock off a few poems
To include with the biography
And the photograph

One Closet
Trina Stolec

Twelve years of our life
packed into one closet:
your suits, my ripped jeans,
broken computers,
stained glass windows you
had to have, but
never used.
I pull out baby dresses –
yellowed lace and dusty ruffles.
The silent room fills
with the memory of you
crawling across the floor
in pursuit of chubby legs which
hadn't developed the coordination to run.
She'd grab my arms,
we'd run away from you
laughing.
We giggled
when you caught us.

Your voice echoes up the stairs –
asks if I need the computer.
I yell an answer.
Dust settles on the rug.
I pack twelve years of our life
back into one closet.

Motel Interlude
Cathleen Allyn Conway

What if instead of just driving past,
sniggering at the lobby's mod décor
of dripping electric blue ceiling lights
and walls of geometric mirrors,

we stopped, paid our fifteen bucks,
handed the cranky receptionist our IDs,
and entered one of those dingy rooms
of matted carpets and red velour?

I'd even make the first move, warm you up
with my mouth, purr as you gasp.
We could feed quarters into the Magic Fingers
to fuck on the vibrating bed's dirty sheets,

and when we were both ready, I'd guide you into me,
deflowering one another in a burst of blood, milk, spit

...instead of just talking about it.

Washerwoman
Joe Gianotti

Shirts folded, fresh, crisp,
stacked in a blue plastic basket,
a look like the newly purchased.
I would hook the brow of the basket
onto the waist of my pants and belt,
and balance it on my hip,
as I struggled out her skinny doorway,
coerced more narrow by her wot not
and its made-in-Hong Kong,
dime-store, antiques.

My basket filled with clothes
that never saw the machine
before they found the tub.
She scrubbed the grass and dirt and stain
from the cuffs of my pants,
the sweat from the collars of my shirts,
the white back into my gym socks.
With forever withered hands,
a bar of lye soap,
a metal washing board,
and Depression pride,
she alchemized old into new.

She stood almost everyday in her basement,
to knead the wash, to sow the laundry.
I would often hear her deplore the dishes
or ignore the dusting,

but she never lamented the laundry.

I get dressed now in the clothes of my making.
They do not feel right.
They do not look right.
They are not right.
I cannot plait her concentrated crease.
I cannot recreate the fastidiousness of her folds.

Already, I have found a cracked button
on the wallet side pocket of a pair of pants.
I could not fasten the clasp,
and, at age 37,
I felt surprise at the newness of this experience.

I have learned, in these long eight months,
to feel shame for ever giving her
the grass stained knees of my childhood
or the socks folded inside out from my carelessness.

Late Night Burritos
Joe Gianotti

Sunday creeps toward us
as we barhop on a Saturday night.
We swallow mass quantities
of juniper berries, coriander, saffron,
of grapes, sorghum, molasses.
The single malt. The blended.
Dark spaces roll together.
Songs play forever.
The clink of whiskey glasses
mixes with billiard breaks.

At 3 a.m.,
burritos. We must have burritos.
And the burritos must be plump
with steak and lettuce and tomatoes,
soaked in juice that will
run from our impetuous lips,
dribbling down our chins,
only to be wiped up again and again
with the ass of the tortilla.

We stagger to the diner
and read the menus
with eyes as glossy as window clings.
We talk loudly,
and we grunt laughing noises
with mouths full of food.

Outside, we light cigarettes
and strut like caudillos,
but pieces of cheese and shell
grapple to our uniform oxfords.

In the morning,
we will spread ourselves
throughout the city,
like forager bees to nectar sources,
jobs to perform for our weekend queen.

Grocery Girl
Joe Gianotti

You wore your brother's army/navy surplus field jacket,
green and unzipped,
and your younger sister's yellow tank top.
You sprouted short, scraggly hair,
and long, tanned legs
that burst out of scuffed tennis shoes
like swirling search lights
at a strip club's grand opening
that shone into your white washed denim shorts.
Striped gym socks scrunched around your ankles.
No bra.

You waited a long time to come into my home.
You reconnoitered through acquaintances,
sent treaties by way of counselors,
gained invitation via lieutenants.
You walked through my front gate
all ribboned and bowed,
and I carelessly undid you.
You gnawed on me for hours,
greedily worked me with your canines,
lustily turned me with your forepaws.

And in the end,
it took me twenty years to write this poem.

when lost in innocence
Bree

i saw lion faces in each
of the leaves of this tree

hundreds of them,

and each of the faces, the glances
they made, being humble and
strong and what i wanted to be.

We Are All Orange
Bree

for you, Gearity Elementary

They asked me to speak to you about poetry,
diversity. To say we are the same would cause
scandal, controversy. To say whether we are
sisters or brothers, adults or coming up, we're
all corrupt and are corrupted, to say we start
out right even if we are interrupted, to say
we start out downright perfect,
o Say, somewhere someone loves us,
even if its one person who isnt nuts.

To say we start out fresh and gather dust,
to say we have the world in the palm that grows
outside our huts, in the hassles happening outside
our castles, to suggest the streets we walk to stand
in line for the bus or limo, tractor, compact, Hummer,
trailer, SUV, to suggest those streets are any less
than what makes us us.

So so we grow every day we listen up
to the traffic (o say can we?)

Beats in tires squeal ling
drums in the weathermen flying in
the copters, songs in the ivy
and the pattern that it makes
on buildings, sweet and ill feeling

climb up.

What climbs on us? What jive shucks?
Black yellow brown red and white fingers grip a
pen or punch a pad to write. Man woman child
and in between copy down to share what theyve
seen. Whether voices carry on with fictions
or speak personal truths, to say we are
the same is contra(diction).

Diction means to speak. Make it proud.
Make it from the heart so we can see we.
So you can see that you and i are me.

Yeah right, you and what army?

The power of the pen the sword cuts down the
might of buildings, businesses, mayors, contracts,
cancers, districts. Color blinds, venetian opening
consciousness like traffic widens, power of the
pen so much stronger than living in one.

Yoo hoo did you say diversity?
To say youre me would cause a scandal.
Difference is who it is that just loves us
cause they give the boost so you and i
can know whats what—
blue green violet and orange.

In 6th grade the joke was nothing
rhymes with orange, but im not listening.

When fruit is just been washed its glistening.
When i speak my rhymes whole hoards
are listening, so when they say
'can't' you rhyme,
you spit orange.

Ohios in the foothills of mountain o ranges
we climb and descend, Cleveland, we cant
rhyme with us. In the sunset we are orange,
all of us. When the sun sets another day
makes history. We start out right, we climb we.

we'll be on our way home when the smoke whispers in the sky
Ross Vassilev

these red brick walls
these grey streets that I've walked up and down
for so many years
with the sparrows at sunrise
under afternoon drizzle
with sunshine falling on blankets of snow
and I remember the last 20 years
like an old great river that never stops
like a short walk to the end of the street
and I remember that old hobo
who asked me what time it was
and I told him and he said
Is that all?
and then like Bob Dylan
he walked away and disappeared
among the streetlights
and the dusk.

say what?
Ross Vassilev

there'll be no white elephants
crossing my path

the "I" may be an illusion
but all poets seek fame and glory

the "I" may be an illusion
but the memories in my head seem real

and the rage and the fury
are real enough

I'll lay myself down in the nectar
of the black rose of night

and maybe the Gods will visit me
bearing a thousand gifts

or maybe just one gift
red as a plum

and when the world finally drowns
in the last great flood

maybe my salvation will lie
in the suffering of others.

semper fi
Ross Vassilev

American war criminals
going off to kill
the newest Indians
searching for imaginary
weapons of mass destruction
armed with real ones
like white phosphorus
depleted uranium
and enough lies
to fill a whole country
with mad killer clowns

I'd pelt you with
anarchist tomatoes
but you'd lock me up
without trial
in Gitmo, that once
beautiful place
that you stole
from the people of Cuba
who just want to be
left in peace

white Americans,
I spit on you
and your sheer animal
bloodlust
on the oligarchs who

profit from your wars
and the idiots
who fight them.

trinity
Ross Vassilev

the veterans
are coming home
again
as I put a quarter
in the soda machine
and remember a poster
I once saw of a
gorgeous redhead
in a black dress
the veterans
are always coming home
from the latest war
and God must spend
a lot of time
jerking off
while people are busy
killing each other
and giving each
other medals
and somewhere
out in the desert
lies the hollow skull
of a yesterday cow
as dull and oblivious
and dessicated
as the bull-brained
mob parading
down the street

behind me
a Georgia O'Keefe
cow skull
a sacred-cow skull
with a yellow rose
in one hollow
eye
calling out
across
the desert night.

Sunday Morning
Scot Young

Buster

redbone hound
sleeps soundly
on the front porch
stretched out taking
in the morning sun
dreaming
of the next hunt

you are in the house
frying bacon
making scratch biscuits
maple flavor
drifts through
the open window
you sing Streisand
it sounds good
paired against
these Ozark hills
almost spiritual
bringing culture
to this holler.

blue car stops
in driveway
jehovah's witness
steps out

begins the conversation
Ol' Buster raises up
barks slightly
looks him straight
in the eye
and begins
licking his balls
like any good
coon hound
would do
on a perfect
Sunday morning.

mother's bucket
Scot Young

we often dream the dreams
we'll forget in the morning
but each night
you hover above us
angel wings touching
the tip of the moon
holding your bucket of blue stars
dropping each one gently

–they protect us
you make sure of that
and somewhere in the city
a young mother blows bubbles
with their child for the first time

i wonder if you were dropping
blue stars there too?

Poetry 101
Scot Young

i taught a poetry class
to your abused
broken & neglected
children and started to give
them metaphors
similes &
personification
but they knew figurative language
well enough and tried to wear
the face of normal wanting
to be like other kids
—tried to hide the scars
with just inked tattoos and too much
mascara

they read their poems
of incest
of rape
of beatings
of parents in prison
of foster homes
of being hooked on meth made
down a dead end county road
of how life is not suppose
to be at age 15
they learned that giving
human characteristics
to inanimate objects

sometimes lessened the pain

but i changed my lesson
plan when one of them said

hey teach
what is good poetry?

i suppose it is keeping
your wounds close
to the surface so they can heal
quicker

is that it?

on most days
it is

Generation Zero
Walter Beck

"I hope I die before I get old." –Roger Daltery

We've been zeroed in on since we were little kids;
1997 in Mississippi and Kentucky,
1998 in Arkansas, Oregon and Pennsylvania,

And the bloody rampage in Colorado
1999.

Not even leaving our hometowns for college
Could shield us,

As the blood ran thick in Virginia
In 2007.

It's enough that our friends lie buried in a desert,
Fighting for a cause
None of us knew.

But we've lived our lives
With someone zeroing in on us,
On the Second floor,
On the Second street,
In the Second room

With a Second perpetrator.

The preachers gnashed their teeth for the cameras

Saying they wept for our friends,
But their wringing hands
Pried themselves apart
To collect the donations;

Blood money for our friends
To "bring morality back".

But did all their blood money
And their wailing about morality

Save even one of our friends?

Our friends lie buried in the hallways;
Swept under the rug
By a river of blood money
Flowing from the lobby of the Capitol.

They say freedom isn't free
And so many of our friends lie buried

But still not one dead tyrant.

Now we're looking at 30
And after being zeroed in on
Since we were little kids

We have grown old before our time.

I Can Still See You (A Life of Dreams)
Walter Beck

I can still see you,
In your slinky evening gown
Strutting down the stage
Like the queen of all creation.

And I can still you,
With my red fedora tipped to the crowd
To collect your tips.
And I remember
As you slipped a cigarette into my lip.

Yes, I can still see you too,
Your pale brown skin
Caressing me,
Tempting me.
Are my old roommates jealous
Of your fondness of me?

I can still see you,
Laughing at my Lenny Bruce records
In your dirty bohemian apartment.
Your work splashed across your walls,
Did you ever paint a picture of me?

I can still see all of you,
In the early morning hours
When the blues stretches out to the sunrise.

The Wind Forgets My Name
Walter Beck

Stuck in a gray stone building eight hours a day
And a single-story brick house at night;
The wind forgets my name.

She forgets my name,
Because I no longer dance in her every night.
A pack of cheap smokes
And good tunes blasting out of a radio,
Speeding in her embrace;
Knowing I, knowing we
Were living in her.

The wind forgets my name
As I grow cold like a bag of ashes
Hung on display.
Shuffled in and out
Amongst people with fast hands
But slow minds.

The wind forgets my name.
She turns her back on me
As my spine is crushed
Under threats from a bald-headed Spanish god;

She can't bear to see me limp.

The wind forgets my name,
Only puffing by with a brief hello

Spoken by people
From better days.

The wind forgets my name,
Only recognizing me
When the moon draws high
And I strut on stage
With that frenzied look in my eyes

She remembers from better days.

Death of a Generation
Walter Beck

We got guts
Protruding over our neat, pressed jeans.
We're no longer junkie thin
From a diet of ramen noodles and cheap beer,
Strutting around in tattered denim
Itching to torch the world.

We're buried
Under thousands of dollars of debt,
For degrees that don't seem to be worth the university president's signature.
We believed that school was the ticket
To keep from becoming minimum wage slaves;

That beautiful lie vanished
After we stepped into the line for a Wal-Mart job.

We're dead before we're thirty,
Toasting to glory days that never really seemed to exist.
Dead before we're thirty,
Having consigned ourselves to forty years in the waiting room
For an American dream

That will never come for the likes of us.

3:38am at the truck stop
Justin Hyde

he sat down
at the little
u-shaped counter
up front

tried lighting
a cigarette
but kept dropping
the matches.

his skin
was the color of
skim milk.

you alright?
waitress
asked.

having
a heart attack,
his voice came
like a skeleton

sweat dripping
off his chin.

waitress
ran to the phone

for an
ambulance.

want me
to help you
onto the floor?
i asked him.

just light my cigarette
will you,
he said
body stiff
as a bent nail.

he took off
an old silver watch
with a white face
slid it towards me
along with his cellphone
and wallet.

you tell her
i remember that night
under the stars
at lake red rock,
he said

made me
write it
on a napkin
along with his

wife's phone number
down in
joplin missouri.

the man in the back who ran the label machine
Justin Hyde

dave was having problems with his kid:
twenty-three years old
running through jobs
two owi's.

you can't talk to him
thinks he wrote the book,
dave told me once
at lunch break.

the janitor paul
told me
it was dave's own making
said the kid
came to live with dave
when he was
four years old
after his mother died.
said dave told him
how the kid
would try to snuggle with him
on the couch
but dave would
push him away.

when a kid wants to snuggle
you don't push em away
you open your arms

wide as you can
then wider still,
paul said
eyes twisted
with hurt.

paul had a
fifth grade education.

he used the word nigger
and had a payee
to keep track of his money.

but sometimes
he made more sense
than the rest of us.

grocery shopping for the schizophrenics
Justin Hyde

my first job out of college
was as a mental health counselor
at a non-profit
in iowa city

four clients
lived at the residential house
on birch street

every wednesday
i had 150$
to buy groceries

i never made a budget
but i always got what was needed
with enough left over for

james' king size snickers
marlboro reds for carol
kim's tube of cookie dough

and a cosmo
for sarah

because she was studying to be an actress
in hollywood
for when god stopped fucking with her.

Sheltering Sheila
Brian Fugett

5:57a.m.
The motel room
is still thick
with shadows.

I linger in bed,
pinned down
by the gravity
of a throbbing
hangover.

The distant sounds
of the highway
filter in
on the breeze
as Sheila gazes
out the window
huddled over
a cigarette.

"Baby killer!"
a voice shrieks
from the next room.
A door slams
& an argument erupts.

Sheila flicks
her cigarette

out the window
& cups her palms
around her ears.

"Sometimes, when
it's really quiet,
my hands sound
like the ocean,"
she says, focusing
her eyes
on the horizon.

This is the Damn Poem
Brian Fugett

This is the poem procured from the excrement
of Oprah Winfrey's book of the month
This is the poem found coursing through the
irritable bowels of a Shetland pony
This is the poem hijacked from sweat drenched
bar stools and strangled rectal meat
This is the poem gleaned from the pituitary gland
of a morbidly obese beautician

This is the poem brimming with
intimacy issues and palm sweat
This is the poem full of tube sock ejaculate
This is the poem that tickles your throat
like a slow tongue swallow
This is the poem forged from projectile vomit
and feminine itch products
This is the poem supplemented with
big-breasted sluts in gangbang action
This is the poem that bleeds on the carpet
every time you read it upside down
This is the poem wilting in the rusted-out trunk
of a '76 Chevy Nova
This is the poem that tastes like
a "no money back" guarantee

This is the DAMN poem
no one will publish.

Peristalsis in the Bowels of Downtown
Brian Fugett

all up & down
5th street there are
peep shows
coffee shops
liquor stores
& fresh tattoos that glow
on the pale
february bleached flesh
of girls
& all the skinny caramel lattes
are clutched too tight
even though they are hotter than
the august pavement
& everywhere you go
along east 3rd street
the cell phones are screaming
to be released from
all of the pockets
purses
& glove compartment coffins
while a roving pack of mimes
stalk the corner of 4th & main
peddling
thespian nightmares
in a symphony of silence
so loud
it sounds like propaganda
& all the yellow

slowly leaks
from the sun
as i sit in the café
across the street
murdering myself
one cigarette
at a time.

The Deterioration of My Handwriting
Bill Yarrow

I got a D in handwriting in the third grade.
I'm an old man now.
That failure continues to haunt me.

I saved all the letters from girls who said they loved me.
As I look back on them, I can tell the ones I liked
by the handwriting alone.

When that girl from Princeton Junction drew hearts to dot her "i"s
I lost interest immediately.
I also hated her large loopy cursive.

I cared little about scent, sealing wax, color or watermark.
Tiny precise script in real ink on elegant paper
gave me deep pleasure.

As I became a man, I worked on improving my handwriting.
Its sloppiness infuriated me.
It was too revelatory.

I stopped writing letters on pilfered bank deposit slips.
I sprung for better pens.
I adjusted my thinking to maximize the purity of my hand.

The better my handwriting got, the straighter I stood.
I filled a thousand avid notebooks. I took a mistress.
My handwriting became my immaculate paramour.

But recently I've noticed I can no longer hold a pen with brash
panache. My journals have become slapdash
embarrassments. I open them to random

ugliness. I don't have the solace of the integrity of the handwritten
alphabet. Sterile emails in obvious fonts assail me.
I don't fall in love anymore.

I wish my hands could still carve the cuneiform of beauty
on the waxy emptiness of thought, but all that's left me.
What is left me? The precise boredom of processing processed keys.

I Am Not a Corpse
Bill Yarrow

A corpse cannot cry. A man who cannot
cry is a corpse. I am not a corpse, alas.
If I were, I'd be in a suit. If I were, I'd be
the main event, the center of attention.
All the vultures would be my friends.
All the grubs would love me.
I'd be in touch with dirt, the slime divine,
the slutty mud, the lovely muck.
Or something a little more incendiary,
a mite more vital, robust, fume inducing.
Back to my thesis: a corpse cannot cry.
The tear ducts are bankrupt in death.
There's a haughtiness that sets in, that
sees in raw emotion its sour avatar.

Before the Door
Bill Yarrow

You just can't believe your key
won't open the front door anymore.
Determined to prove reality wrong,
you board a flight to Budapest
and walk wet streets in search of
a keyhole you're convinced exists.
And when you find it on the side door
of the Nicolae Bakery, your wry heart,
rapt with vindication, laughs heartily.
The key works! It really works!
But you don't enter. You don't dare.
Time passes. The seasons alter.
The world gives birth to triplets.
People drop hot pennies into your hat.

You Should've Listened When I Told You Not to Play with Them Guns in the First Place
Julie Demoff-Larson

Boys. Young boys.
Convinced by those paid to teach them,
by parents who never encouraged them,
that they have no options
except the American PTSD dream—
taking them from burnt-out,
rotgut towns
to secluded bases.

Alienation.

Pledge. Salute. Submit.
Breaking down the individual,
cloning defensive response times,
making machines out of flesh.

Airborne protocol,
  you ain't no jump chump,
you a Mud Dog.

Georgia swamp qualified—
down on elbows,
uniform weapon clip full—
practice creates
digitized sharp shooter black-out eyes.

Ready?

Hell ya, I'm ready!

Pumped up on adrenalin
and DoD cocktail,
they ship you out
sight unseen,
one by one.

There—
the sand oozes like oil
through cracks between your fingers;
cave monsters inhabit
your shallow dreams.
Busting down doors,
quick and agile
as when pretending to be Kato
while watching reruns
in the privacy of your bedroom—
when you were a boy.

Weaving in and out
centuries-old stone mazes,
behind every corner
justification of ideologies
waiting
to get you first
as extreme emotional ties and
beliefs outdated
create paranoia—a stealth operator.

Trigger-happy fingers.

On approach you choke,
conviction shatters
the eye of an unarmed man.

Abandoning the regiment
for a day ride
with commanding officers,
buddies blow up at the checkpoint.
Surviving morphs your brain—

Guilt.

Home—
sitting on the roof
yelling beyond the trees,
Can't you see them?
Tripping,
reality playing out
in mutated thought.
Diagnosed:
white patched
shell-shocked
frontal lobes,
processing like eighty year old dementia patients
laid up at the V.A.

The V.A.—
where men like you—
concealed
and never debriefed—
feed your body

pill-cocktails
equivalent of strychnine,
twisting memory and
time continuum
into one mass-murder
 in your head.

When late nights alone
standing in the hallway of our parents' home,
while they sleep
Jack Daniels races
through your boiling blood,
forehead pressed
firm against the wall,
flicking the light
 off and on,
       off and on,
like a glitched replay.
Reciting credentials and
what you did and
what they won't allow
you to do now,
deemed too unfit
to be bothered with...

You were a soldier once, Mud Dog.
Soldier on.

When You are a Thousand Miles from Home
Julie Demoff-Larson

She didn't say much,
 to stop or to go
before she touched my skin
with her fingertips,
or when her tongue touched my lips
as we sat on the driftwood
at Surfside beach.

She didn't trouble herself
with right or wrong,
or if my father thought she had no morals,
concerned only with the surf
moving over our feet
tired from the walk from the highway,
weighed down
by the forty pound packs we carried
for a thousand miles
from home.

We left home with those little Mother Mary's in our pockets,
but the guilt she provided didn't stop us
or the husband resting in the tent
down the beach
because, after all, it started as
me, watching her
dance like a ballerina
at my wedding
and I knew it was a matter of time

before she brought me in—
and only a matter of a moment
before she would bring him in too.

crank
Tom Janikowski

clamor, climb-on, claim it
and sail on through to a desperate end
holding fast to drip-down,
trickle-down, beaten-down
self-suffering alibi
$C_{10} H_{15} N$

methdream methking
walter with the white spitfleck thing
whitepasty saliva paste stuck to a dried leatherdried boca
boca, walter, is what they call the mouth, you know

but methking methdream you suck that red fruit punch
like a hungry, thirsty, slobbering idiot
(god I hate to see it say it think it but I do)
red sugarsweet fruit punch jacks up that bloodsugar
you stand there with the red sugarsweet fruit punch
dripping down your dark leatherskin face
and I know I can't stand it but I watch it everyday
red motherloverslobber methking methstream
suck and suck that red sugarsweet fruit punch
like a fruit punch whore sucking down that
honeysweet sugarsweet red methdream
alive your leatherskin fries and dies and looks like feces
crapped out of the system
smelling like a boot dirtyboot that stands and sweats
sweats that red honeysweet sugarsweet
red honey nectar suck you like a vein sucked dry
$C_{10} H_{15} N$

god how I wish I could draw a picture
and show the world that leatherskin methking
with the white spitfleck thing
whitepasty saliva paste
crusty white in the corner of his eye
dry swollen tongue and crustmouth empty
$C_{10} H_{15} N$

boca, clamor, climb-on, claim it
and sail on through to a desperate end
walter, have some self-respect
show some dignity
that damned white priest
with the starchwhite collar
starchwhite hand holding out
and holding tight
starchwhite bastard priest
thinks he knows so much
starchwhite faces leatherskin feces face
and starchwhite priest
the red honeynectar never calls
that starchwhite priest
starchwhite
priest
dies
and dies
again
and again
dies

clamor, climb-on, claim it
and sail on through to a desperate end
while walter sucks the red honeysweet nectar
and you stand there with
the red sugarsweet fruit punch
dripping down your dark leatherskin face

there have been better days
Tom Janikowski

A priceless pushcart wobbles to the front of the dream and a smooth, smooth sailor trains his hair to talk. Talk, Skeezix, talk – you'll need it soon. That smooth, smooth sailor walks a fine line, a cautious line, a line that traces a path behind the priceless pushcart, wobbling to the beat of his heart. The pushcart wobbles. The sailor is smooth, smooth. And the sailor walks a fine, fine line – a cautious line, some would say (I said it) behind that priceless pushcart.

"Snickering idiots," says the sailor (the smooth, smooth sailor) as he walks that fine and cautious line. The idiots don't want what the sailor is selling, and they only want to see the pushcart fall to pieces (we always want to see the pushcart fall to pieces, you know) (there was that time that the golden pushcart with the vapor-charged, high ding-dang, pooch-ed octane rip-snort engine came all to pieces in the back stretch of a mid-life crisis and the people cheered, they cheered, they cheered. They put down their soft-core pornography and their microwaved lava cakes and their television remote-controls and they cheered, they cheered, they cheered. The sailor who happened to be behind that particular golden pushcart with the vapor-charged, high ding-dang, pooch-ed octane rip-snort engine was dismembered and covered in unspeakable things. And the people cheered, they cheered, they cheered).

The snickering idiots mocked the one true and living God. They stuffed their faces with ground beef and melted cheese and the ubiquitous sesame-seed bun. They kept hollering that they knew better, because they were bloody well smarter than all the generations that had gone before. Because of their great, advanced intelligence, they knew that they knew better, and they could laugh at the neanderthals who lit their candles and shook their beads and knelt on the hard, hard ground and tried to love one another. The snickering idiots were smart. They just continued to shove the ground beef full of antibiotics and pasteurized cow-shit into their greedy little holes and they pushed away the books that their grandparents had left to them, and they rushed around and screamed that they had no free time and had to rush to get little Justin and little Kayla to the soccer practice and the swimming practice and the band practice and the fornication practice and they screamed they had no free time and they sat for hours in front of a box with a talking head telling them what to believe, and they waited to see the pushcart fall to pieces, so that they could cheer, cheer, cheer, the way they had the time that the golden pushcart with the vapor-charged, high ding-dang, pooch-ed octane rip-snort engine came all to pieces. Bastard snickering idiots mocking the true and living God. I'd like to wipe some of that dung – that stinking, stinking dung from your sacrifices onto the faces of your talking head high-priests in the snickering idiot box with the antibiotic ground beef-engine roaring to life in the back stretch, screaming to speak over the screams and the shouts as you copulate with the idiot box in your great, advanced modern intelligence as you kill yourself with a text-messaged social media stake through your own throbbing, wobbling, antibiotic advertised-shitty beef-grease gobbling heart.

The sailor lives. And the sailor and me, we're sick of it.

Practice
Kayla Greenwell

I was sitting at the kitchen table
spitting watermelon seeds into the trash

when the memory of your hands wrapped
around my neck and I choked them back down,
fearing the brick wall above the stove
and all its tiny imperfections.

you taught me that a woman was a target
the red rings inside of me
burned to liquid and converged.

any girls is all girls and I am
the girl triumphant.
So I will dig my teeth into my bones
until I cannot tell one
from the other.

the 9 o'clock news is on tv
my brother is taking his second shower today
the one you said he needed but
forgot to add that it was so you
could get me alone.

What if I had known enough
to bite your tongue instead
of my own?

you wanted more of me.
more fingers curling, eyes darting
trying to avoid what you want me to see
more sweat in the summer time than I know what
to do with.

my skin dissolves, leaving my muscles
deconstructing and reconnecting
against the natural laws until
I am unrecognizable.
A monster trapped behind the lazy-boy chair.

my synapses snap no more and my
blood does not slow but is
Forced to halt completely
and i ask you
politely, quietly   to stop.

Certified Outlaw
Tim Murray

what does it mean to be an
outlaw poet?

is there one holy all-
encompassing definition that
adequately covers all of the
literary bases and makes
everyone who wears the badge
of outlaw grin with
crooked teeth?

am i an outlaw by virtue of
being broke no joke?

am i an outlaw because
poetry magazine return my
manuscripts no thanks kid
keep dreaming?

to be an outlaw do i need to
depict the bar scene and
fictitious braggart drunken
brawls?

to be an outlaw do i need to
always get the chick and
lick pussy and/or suck cock?

to be an outlaw do i need a rap
sheet?

must i shun the university and
set fire to robert
frost?

should an outlaw
rent/own/charge/borrow or file
bankruptcy?

does the fact that i do not own
a cell phone suffice
for official outlaw status?

does shopping at walmart
render one ineligible for
the outlaw bumper sticker?

is the term outlaw defined by
the type of vehicle that
you drive/pedal/push/or
borrow?

must i smoke
cigarettes/grass/crack/or
the aforementioned cock
in order to be a
good outlaw?

my critique of ezra pound, to

say the least, is that
his methods of poetic
construction are pretentious
and
outdated. i MUST be an outlaw
poet!

is outlaw a mere literary
genre/label/mindset/or way
of life?

do outlaws enjoy drive-in
movies/anal beads/golden
showers/or being on the
receiving end of a hot carl?

do outlaws
poop/pee/sneeze/cough/cackle/
groan/cry/vote/or drink
kool-aid?

i was once a member of the
socialist party and prior
to that i was an ardent
mustachioed fascist. does my
record of political restlessness
hinder my ability to
fly the outlaw banner?

must i give up my infatuation
with the chicago white

sox in order for my
club outlaw
membership application
to qualify?

is the church of outlaws a
religion?
must i proclaim that the
literary apocalypse is upon
us?
where do rod mckuen
and john burroughs fit in?

does having offspring handicap
one's ranking in the
world of outlaws?

do outlaws pet kittens/eat
watermelon/tie their
shoes or phone their mothers?

is it up to me to choose the
title of outlaw or do i
have to wait around for it to
choose me?

perhaps there is a committee
that is busy assessing my
outlaw
credentials/qualifications/and
credit history.

perhaps they will send me a
certified letter of
approval.

i'm still waiting for the postman.

God Lost His Pet Gopher in a Patch of Roiling Gray Clouds Hovering Over Miller Beach Indiana
Tim Murray

I once saw an old WW1 biplane pulling a messy
love triangle among a family of trapeze artists across the clear
summer skies above Lake Michigan
fighting a cat for its last morsel of food is always a dickless move
no matter how you slice it
now I'm sifting through Ultimate Warrior videos happily lost
in the land of the human heart disguised as Alfred Hitchcock
a very special thanks to Behemoth you old son of a gun!
the sucking titty babies will eventually come looking for me
until then I've landed a true bucket list dream job
my task is to walk around all day crying in public
while dragging a partially eaten buffalo behind me on a leash
rest assured darlin' our non-negotiable return flight will eventually leave
this mercurial world ruled by the omnipotently indifferent ghost of a
Gaylord Perry spit ball hurling through the clouds at all hours dripping
Vaseline in our eyes from a razor blade slit in the Emory board red sky

Part 1
Tim Murray

Thru blind birth luck
I live in Indiana
Frozen crossroads of the American conundrum
Under the legalized gusts
Of steel mill exhausts
Where the mercury-laced waters
Of Lake Michigan lap in the north
Where vinyl nightmare houses replace
Crops in fields
Where boys spend summers pissing from trees
In Dinosaur Ditch
Where grandma's iron kitchen skillet
First received its golden commandment from heaven
Where daddy walked the brief brawling streets
Of youth
Where Mrs. Burton offered phantom treats
From Halloween tray of neighborhood lore
Where Mr. Berkley sat with coke plant
Emphysema cough
Where Red Cunningham lost his arm to the
Alligator machinery of industry
Where summer lasts for two hours in July
Then returns to comforting gray chilled skies
Where Tina was snuffed out at 19
Stabbed and discarded like a sack of trash
Still no suspects in sight
Where teens crack garage doors to vent
Afternoon bong coughs

Where there is a church and a bar on
Every corner espousing liquid heaven escape
Where I often think of myself blessed and trapped
Third generation familiar with the sounds of these bleeding
Streets its inhabitants visions dreams changes
Bursting with a tragic
Fragile and hopeful rebirth

Mark James Andrews lives and writes one mile outside the city limits of Detroit most of the time and has been many times published, many times rejected. He is the author of a couple of poetry chapbooks *Punkpomes pleeze* (Jesus' Home Run Press) and *Burning Trash* (Pudding House), a flash fiction collection *Compendium 20/20* (Deadly Chaps) and a poetry CD *Brylcreem Sandwich* with Tom Brzezina.

James Babbs continues to live and write from the same small Illinois town where he grew up. James has published hundreds of poems over the past thirty years, both, in print and online. He is the author of *Disturbing The Light* (2013) & *The Weight of Invisible Things* (2013).

Walter Beck is from Avon, IN and is a graduate of Indiana State University. His work has appeared in various journals and rags throughout the country and even a few internationally. He has a growing cult following for his intense verse and unorthodox live performances. He is one of the co-hosts of a weekly radio show called "The Rainbow Asylum" on the Outright Libertarians Radio Network and writes a weekly column for *Omnibus Journal* titled "Walt's Soapbox."

David Blaine, the writer not the magician, lives and works with his family in rural Michigan. David has had poetry, prose, essays, reviews and interviews published widely online, on air, and in print. His last book of poems, *Antisocial*, was published in 2009 by Outsider Writers Press. David is presently collecting stories best described as flash non-fiction. You can sample these at *Tell Me Your Story*. http://tellittomebrother.blogspot.com/

Sirenna Blas lives in the Chicagoland area. While she does write poetry, her main focus is on short fiction, which has been published in journals such as *Mangrove, Petrichor, The Bicycle Review, Broad* and *Red Ochre Lit*. She has a B.A. in English Literature but currently works with her hands.

April Michelle Bratten lives in North Dakota. Her work has appeared or is forthcoming in *Thrush Poetry Journal, Zone 3, Southeast Review, Gargoyle*, and others. She is the editor of *Up the Staircase Quarterly*.

Bree is a poet and founder of Green Panda Press which has produced poetry and art chapbooks, anthologies, broads and sundry in the small press since 2001. Her work has appeared in *Arthur, Big Bridge, Ecstatic Peace, The City, Whiskey Island* and numerous small mags. Her books include *Let Cupid Know* (Ronin Press, UK 2012), *A Leg to Stand On* (Green Panda 2013), *Laying Pans* (Ecstatic Peace, MA 2009), *was chicken trax amid sparrows tread* (Temple Books 2009), and other memoirs and poesy. She puts out *Least Bittern Books* from the farmland of Henry County, KY.

Judy L. Brekke bio: Born in and again resides in Minnesota (spent between 1969 and 1982 in the Bay Area). A co-editor of JUICE with the late Stephen S. Morse, (first as a print magazine then an e-zine). She has worked with children all her life in early childhood education. Wrote and illustrated a child's book of poetry in 1981- never submitted - it rests on her bookshelf. Completed a book of poetry with Stephen S. Morse, *Places that Linger*, dedicated to their granddaughter, Willow. Published in numerous small literary magazines both print and on-line. Won the Ina Coolbrith Memorial Poetry Award in 1978 and 1979 with her poems sharing a place in the University of California (Berkeley) Archives.

Craig Cady is a midwest-born poet and performance artist currently based in North Hollywood by way of Brooklyn. He is studying gerontology at USC to design cooperative art-focused retirement communities.

J.J. Campbell (1976 - soon) has given up the farm life and is now trapped in suburbia. He's been widely published over the years, most notably at *Chiron Review, Nerve Cowboy, Thunder Sandwich, Zygote in My Coffee* and *Dead Snakes*. His first full length collection of poetry, *Sofisticated White Trash* (Interior Noise Press), is available wherever you happen to buy books these days. You can find J.J. most days bitching about things only he cares about on his highly entertaining blog, evil delights. (http://evildelights.blogspot.com)

Wanda Morrow Clevenger lives in Hettick, IL – population 200 give or take. She has published over 320 pieces of work in 121 print and electronic publications. Her debut book *This Same Small Town in Each of Us* released in 2011 (Edgar & Lenore's Publishing House). A full-length poetry manuscript is currently stalking unsuspecting publishers. For more info, visit her About Me page: http://about.me/wandamorrowclevenger

Ryder Collins has a novel, *Homegirl!* Her chapbook, *The way the sky was now*, recently won Heavy Feather Review's first fiction chapbook contest. She has a chapbook of poetry entitled, *Orpheus on toast*, and her most recent release *i am hopscotch without hop* is now available from Kleft Jaw Press. Please visit her blog for more http://bignortherngirlgoes.blogspot.com/

Cathleen Allyn Conway is an American-British poet. She is also a journalist, teacher, and academic researching the work of Sylvia Plath. She is editor of *Thank You for Swallowing*, a protest poetry webzine. Her pamphlet *Static Cling* was published in 2012 by Dancing Girl Press. Originally from Chicago, she lives in London with her son, her cats, and her husband, who is disappointingly not John Taylor of Duran Duran.

Juliet Cook is a grotesque glitter witch medusa hybrid brimming with black, grey, silver, purple, and red explosions. Her poetry has appeared in a peculiar multitude of literary publications, recently including *FLAPPERHOUSE, Ghost Proposal, H_NGM_N, ILK,* and *Menacing Hedge.* She is the author of more than thirteen published poetry chapbooks, most recently including *POISONOUS BEAUTYSKULL LOLLIPOP* (Grey Book Press, 2013), *RED DEMOLITION* (Shirt Pocket Press, 2014) and a collaborative chapbook with Robert Cole, *MUTANT NEURON CODEX SWARM* (Hyacinth Girl Press, 2015). Another new collaborative chapbook by Juliet Cook and j/j hastain, *Dive Back Down*, is forthcoming from Dancing Girl Press later in 2015. Cook's first full-length poetry book, *Horrific Confection* was published by BlazeVOX in 2008 and her second full-length poetry book, *Malformed Confetti,* is forthcoming from Crisis Chronicles Press later in 2015. You can find out more at www.JulietCook.weebly.com.

Julie Demoff-Larson is one of the founding editors and currently the Managing Editor at *Blotterature Literary Magazine.* She is the chief organizer and curator of "Small Prestivus," a two-day annual literary festival aimed at promoting the diversity of small presses and the writers they represent. Julie has a B.A. in English Literature from Purdue University. Her dedication to the writing community is second only to family and friends. Her short stories have been published in *Mangrove, Ricochet, Epiphany Magazine* and in *Good Morning, Justice* an anthology from Brine Books Publishing.

Brian Fugett is a member of the slacker, fast food generation that has been branded with an 'X' by that Canadian-born, literary terrorist known as Douglas Coupland. Meanwhile, he sits in his pad all day consuming more oxygen than he's worth. He's been doing it for over 40 years now and has become quite effecient at it. Eating and voiding are the only things he really knows how to do. Between meals and trips to the shitter, he covertly milks

'West Nile Virus' from the tits of pregnant mosquitoes and uses it to butter the toast of local politicians. He is the editor/publisher of *Zygote in My Coffee*.

Joe Gianotti is from Whiting, a small, blue collar town on the fringe of Chicago. He has taught English at Lowell High School for seventeen years. His poetry has been published or is forthcoming in *Steam Ticket: A Third Coast Review, This, Literary Magazine, The Chaffey Review, Folly, Yes, Poetry, Wilderness House Review, Mouse Tales,* and other places. You can follow him on Twitter @jgianotti10.

Kayla Greenwell is probably human, but it's impossible to tell. She writes strange fiction, even stranger non-fiction, and has recently started sticking her fingers in the poetry pie. She works for *Blotterature Literary Magazine* as both the Editor-At-Large and the Blot Lit Reviews Editor. She has 6 cats, but it's cool, because it's not like, in that crazy cat lady way. I mean. At least she thinks it isn't.

Michael D. Grover is a Toledo-based poet, activist, and editor/publisher. He has been published extensively in the small press, is the head poetry editor at *Red Fez Publications*, and has run several successful reading series in Ohio, California, and Florida. He is also a vegetarian and drives a pimp-mobile.

Steven Gulvezan has lived and worked in the Detroit area his entire life. His poems and stories have appeared in publications ranging from *Ellery Queen's Mystery Magazine* to *Underground Voices*. A collection of his poetry is *The Dogs of Paris* (March Street Press).

Justin Hyde currently lives in Iowa, USA.

Tom Janikowski is a Midwestern author who delights in surrealism and symbolism. His poetry, flashes and short stories have appeared online and in print on both sides of the Atlantic, and his forthcoming *Crawford County Sketchbook* (Red Hen Press, August 2015) is a collection of tales set in a rural county somewhere in the deep South. Janikowski is greatly influenced by "Lost Generation" authors such as William Faulkner, F. Scott Fitzgerald and Ernest Hemingway, but he also admits long-standing love affairs with the writing of Kurt Vonnegut and John Updike. He currently works, writes, and mixes cocktails in Davenport, Iowa. Find him at www.tomjanikowski.com

Michele McDannold was the Editor-in-Chief at *Red Fez Publications* for five years and is currently the editor/publisher at Citizens for Decent Literature Press and organizer of the "This Is Poetry" project. Michele's first full-length poetry collection *Stealing the Midnight from a Handful of Days* is now available from Punk Hostage Press. She has an extensive collection of flannel and rubber chicken heads.

Catfish McDaris' most infamous chapbook is *Prying* with Jack Micheline and Charles Bukowski. His best readings were in Paris at the Shakespeare and Co. Bookstore and with Jimmy "the ghost of Hendrix" Spencer in NYC on 42nd St. He's done over 20 chaps in the last 25 years. He's been in the *New York Quarterly, Slipstream, Pearl, Main St. Rag, Café Review, Chiron Review, Zen Tattoo, Wormwood Review, Great Weather For Media*, and *Graffiti* and been nominated for 15 Pushcarts, Best of Net in 2010 and 2013, he won the Uprising Award in 1999, and won the Flash Fiction Contest judged by the U.S. Poet Laureate in 2009. His latest book is a hard cover called *Jupiter Orgasma* from Lulu.com here.

Tim Murray is a lifelong resident of Northwest Indiana. He hosted the Red Fez blogtalk radio show from 2010-2012 and The Tim Murray Variety Show on Project U Radio Network. He was nominated for a Pushcart Prize by NightBallet Press for his poem "Certified Outlaw". His e-chap *What I Did Monday* is available for free download from Ten Pages Press. His chapbook *Dinosaur Ditch* was published by Citizens for Decent Literature Press. He was one of the founding editors of *Blotterature Literary Magazine*.

Josh Olsen is a writer, father, and (former?) teacher from Metro Detroit, by way of LaCrosse, Wisconsin. His latest book, *Such a Good Boy*, is available from all the usual online outlets, and he's currently editing an anthology of professional wrestling themed literature, entitled *Working Stiff*.

Jake Russell has a chapbook titled *Great Conversations, Greater Wasps* released through the ELJ Publications. He also has poems published in the *Emerge Literary Journal* (print edition), the *Open Window Review* and *The Weekenders Magazine*. In creative fiction, he has been published in the *Bellows American Review* and work forthcoming in the Moon Hollow Press. He is currently a Master of Fine Arts student at Wichita State University, studying poetry, and is a reader for *Mojo, Mikrokosmos,* and *Citizens for Decent Literature*.

Matthew Sradeja lives in Toledo, Ohio with his wife Kelly and their cat Eleanor. Matthew has worked in the automotive and glass industries. He started attending open mic poetry readings in 1999. You can find his poems at *CFDL, Full of Crow, Red Fez, Splat Art Magazine* and *ppigpenn*. His poetry has been in print issues of *Toledo Free Press Star, Every Reason Zine, CFDL, ToledoPoetryProject*, and in the book *Broadway Bards First* (2010)

Trina Stolec studied poetry and writing at the Cincinnati School for Creative and Performing Arts, Berea College, and The University of Toledo, but she is mostly self taught by reading other poets. She has had over 170 poems appear in over 50 publications including *Agnieszka's Dowry, ZuZu Petals Quarterly, Thunder Sandwich, Recursive Angel, ken*again,* and *Full of Crow*. Alone or as part of the performance art band Logic Alley, she performs and reads her poetry in many venues including The Columbus Arts Festival, Art O Matic 419 and The Old West End Festival.

Ross Vassilev is a born loser and a poet. He's from Bulgaria but now lives in Ohio??? You can read more of his poems at http://rossvassilev.blog.com.

Robert Vaughan leads writing roundtables at Redoak Writing. His writing has appeared in hundreds of print and online journals. He is a Pushcart Prize nominee. His story, "Ten Notes to the Guy Studying Jujitsu" was a finalist for the Gertrude Stein Award 2013. His story "The Rooms We Rented" was a finalist for the Gertrude Stein Award 2014. He is senior flash fiction editor at *JMWW* and *Lost in Thought* magazines. His chapbooks are *Microtones* (Cervena Barva) and *Diptychs + Triptychs* (Deadly Chaps). His first full-length book is *Addicts and Basements* (Civil Coping Mechanisms). www.robert-vaughan.com

Bill Yarrow is the author of *Blasphemer* (Lit Fest Press 2015), *Pointed Sentences* (BlazeVOX 2012) and four chapbooks. His poems have appeared in many print and online magazines including *Poetry International, RHINO, Contrary, DIAGRAM, FRiGG, THRUSH, Gargoyle,* and *PANK*. He is a Professor of English at Joliet Junior College where he teaches creative writing, Shakespeare, and film.

Scot Young is the editor of the *Rusty Truck* and lives in Missouri.

Susan Yount is the Editor and Publisher of *Arsenic Lobster*, works fulltime at the Associated Press, teaches online workshops at the Rooster Moans and is the founder of Misty Publications. She recently completed graduate studies in poetry at Columbia College in Chicago. Her poetry has recently appeared in several print and online magazines including *Roar, Jet Fuel Review, Booth Journal* and *Menacing Hedge*. Susan is a 2003 recipient of The Lynda Hull Memorial Scholarship in Poetry and in 2010 she was awarded first prize in the 16th Annual Juried Reading competition at The Poetry Center of Chicago. In her spare (!) time she moonlights as madam for the Chicago Poetry Bordello. Visit her here: http://susanyount.tumblr.com/

www.ingramcontent.com/pod-product-compliance
Lightning Source LLC
Chambersburg PA
CBHW020901090426
42736CB00008B/458